Transforming Education with Artificial Intelligence

Franklin Fisher

Published by Amazon KDP

Amazon.com, Inc.

P.O. Box 81226

Seattle, WA 98108-1226

United States.

Cover design by Amazon KDP

Printed by Amazon KDP in the USA

Table of contents

Chapter 1

An Introduction to Artificial Intelligence (AI) in Education

The Genesis of AI

Artificial intelligence (AI) represents the emulation of human intelligence within machines, enabling them to reason like humans and replicate their actions. These machines, spanning from computer software to physical robots, possess the capacity to learn from experiences, adapt to new inputs, and execute tasks that traditionally necessitate human cognitive abilities. Such tasks include problem-solving, language comprehension, pattern recognition, and decision-making.

AI can be classified into two primary categories: narrow AI and general AI. Narrow AI, also termed weak AI, is engineered to fulfill specific tasks, such as facial recognition or online searches. In contrast, general AI, often referred to as strong AI, denotes machines capable of executing any intellectual task performed by humans. While narrow AI is prevalent in contemporary applications, general AI remains largely theoretical, serving as an ongoing research pursuit.

In the realm of education, AI encompasses an array of tools and methodologies, including machine learning, natural language processing, and neural networks. These technologies facilitate the development of intelligent tutoring systems, adaptive learning platforms, automated grading mechanisms, and more, all aimed at augmenting the educational journey for students and educators alike.

Historical Trajectory of AI in Education

The integration of AI into education is not a recent phenomenon but has deep historical roots. Its inception traces back several decades to the initial utilization of computers as educational aids. The narrative unfolds in the 1960s and 1970s, marked by the emergence of early computer-assisted instruction endeavors. A pioneering initiative during this era was the creation of the PLATO (Programmed Logic for Automatic Teaching Operations) system at the University of Illinois. PLATO, among the earliest computer-based educational systems, boasted features like courseware, testing modules, and instructional resources.

As computational technology progressed, educational software evolved in complexity and efficacy. The 1980s and 1990s witnessed the rise of intelligent tutoring systems (ITS), leveraging AI techniques to provide personalized instruction and feedback to learners. Prominent instances include the SCHOLAR system, engaging students in interactive dialogues on diverse subjects, and Carnegie Learning's Cognitive Tutor, employing cognitive models to dynamically guide students through learning tasks.

The early 21st century heralded a significant advancement with the advent of machine learning and big data analytics, facilitating more sophisticated AI applications in education. Learning management systems (LMS) like Blackboard and Moodle began integrating AI-driven features to enrich course delivery and student engagement. Simultaneously, the proliferation of online education platforms such as Khan Academy and Coursera leveraged AI algorithms to offer personalized learning paths and resources.

Contemporary Trends and Innovations

Presently, AI's footprint in education is characterized by swift innovation and a burgeoning array of applications reshaping pedagogical practices. Noteworthy trends encompass:

1. **Personalized Learning**: A pivotal trend propelled by AI, personalized learning employs adaptive learning technologies to tailor educational content based on individual students' strengths, weaknesses, and learning preferences. This personalized approach ensures that students receive instruction optimized for their unique needs, fostering enhanced learning outcomes. Platforms like DreamBox and Knewton exemplify personalized learning through adaptive math programs and customized learning paths across subjects.

2. **Intelligent Tutoring Systems (ITS):** ITS are designed to deliver personalized tutoring experiences to students, leveraging AI to gauge learning progress and provide real-time feedback and guidance. These systems emulate the personalized attention of human tutors, finding application in subjects ranging from mathematics to language arts. Carnegie Learning's MATHia and Duolingo, an AI-powered language

learning app, exemplify the efficacy of ITS.

3. **Automated Grading and Assessment:** AI is revolutionizing assessment through automated grading systems capable of evaluating assignments, essays, and complex problem-solving tasks swiftly and accurately. This not only alleviates the grading burden on educators but also provides instantaneous feedback to students, fostering a more efficient learning cycle. Companies like Gradescope offer AI-driven grading solutions that are increasingly being adopted by educational institutions.

4. **Virtual Classrooms and AI Tutors:** The ascent of virtual classrooms, notably accelerated by the COVID-19 pandemic, has witnessed the integration of AI to facilitate online learning. AI tutors, virtual assistants, and chatbots play pivotal roles in supporting students within virtual learning environments, offering explanations, answering queries, and providing emotional support, thereby enhancing the interactivity and engagement of the online learning experience.

5. **Predictive Analytics:** AI-powered predictive analytics analyze data such as attendance, grades, and engagement metrics to identify at-risk students proactively and intervene before academic challenges escalate. This proactive approach aids in improving retention rates and ensuring student success by preemptively addressing potential hurdles.

6. **Language Translation and Learning:** AI-driven translation tools and language learning apps are breaking down language barriers in education. Platforms like Google Translate and Babbel utilize machine learning to deliver accurate translations and personalized language instruction, democratizing education for non-native speakers.

7. **Content Creation and Curation:** AI assists educators in content creation and curation, with tools like OpenAI's GPT-4 generating educational content, quizzes, and lesson plans tailored to specific requirements. This streamlines content development, saving educators time while ensuring material relevance and currency.

8. **Gamification and AI:** AI-enhanced gamification leverages game-design elements to render learning more engaging, adapting game difficulty and content based on individual student progress. Platforms like Kahoot! and Classcraft integrate AI to gamify education effectively, fostering motivation and participation.

Purpose and Scope of the Book

The overarching objective of this book is to furnish a comprehensive overview of AI's utilization in education, scrutinizing its potential benefits, challenges, and future trajectories. Targeted at educators, administrators, policymakers, and individuals intrigued by the convergence of AI and education, the book endeavors to serve as an invaluable resource.

Scope:

1. **Understanding AI Fundamentals**: The book commences with a primer on AI fundamentals, elucidating its types and capabilities to cater to readers without a technical

background yet keen on comprehending AI's applicability in educational contexts.

2. **Historical Perspectives:** By traversing historical milestones, the book elucidates the evolution of educational technology and AI's gradual integration, offering readers insights into the journey and pivotal junctures shaping AI's role in education.

3. **Current Applications and Trends:** The book delves into the contemporary landscape of AI in education, examining cutting-edge tools, platforms, and methodologies. Each chapter dedicated to specific applications offers detailed insights supported by case studies and real-world examples.

4. **Benefits and Challenges:** A nuanced discourse on AI's advantages in education, such as personalized learning and administrative efficiency, is juxtaposed with discussions on challenges, encompassing ethical considerations, data privacy concerns, and potential biases in AI algorithms.

5. **Future Directions:** The book explores emerging trends and

potential trajectories for AI in education, offering a forward-looking perspective to help readers anticipate and prepare for forthcoming innovations.

6. **Practical Guidance:** For educators and administrators contemplating AI integration, the book furnishes practical advice, best practices, and recommendations for seamless implementation. This encompasses guidance on tool selection, data privacy assurance, and staff training, ensuring effective utilization of AI resources.

By comprehensively exploring these facets, the book endeavors to equip readers with the knowledge and insights requisite for navigating the swiftly evolving landscape of AI in education. Empowered with this understanding, readers can make informed decisions, harness AI's potential, and contribute to advancing educational practices in the digital era.

Chapter 2

Shifting Paradigms in Education Technology

Moving from Conventional Approaches to Digital Learning Spaces

The field of education has undergone a significant metamorphosis from traditional, instructor-centered methodologies to dynamic learning environments empowered by technology. Historically, education followed a structured model where teachers held the primary role as knowledge providers while students remained passive recipients. Classrooms heavily relied on textbooks, chalkboards, and in-person interactions.

Traditional teaching methods emphasized memorization and standardized testing, often neglecting individual learning styles and requirements. Teaching tools mainly comprised printed materials, overhead projectors, and physical aids in subjects like mathematics and science. While effective to some extent, these methods were constrained in their capacity to offer personalized learning experiences.

The advent of the digital age in the late 20th and early 21st centuries ushered in significant changes. Computers and the internet enabled novel forms of educational delivery and content dissemination, giving rise to digital classrooms. These classrooms integrate digital devices, online resources, and interactive platforms.

Digital learning environments leverage technology to create more captivating and adaptable educational settings. Chalkboards have been replaced by interactive whiteboards, enabling dynamic presentations and interactive lessons. Computers and tablets have become commonplace, granting students access to a vast array of online resources and educational software. This transition also facilitated remote learning, broadening access to education irrespective of geographical barriers.

A paramount advantage of digital classrooms lies in their ability to customize education to meet individual student needs. Adaptive learning technologies and personalized learning plans have emerged, allowing educators to accommodate diverse learning paces and styles. Digital platforms also foster collaborative learning through features such as forums, video conferencing, and shared documents.

Early Innovations in Educational Software and Tools The journey of educational technology commenced with the development of early educational software and tools. In the 1960s and 1970s, computer-assisted instruction (CAI) systems pioneered the incorporation of computers into educational settings. These systems provided programmed learning experiences through computers, offering a new avenue for delivering instructional content.

A pioneering project during this period was the PLATO (Programmed Logic for Automatic Teaching Operations) system, originating from the University of Illinois in the early 1960s. PLATO stood as one of the earliest computer-based education systems, featuring courseware, testing modules, and rudimentary social networking functions. It covered a wide array of subjects, ranging from mathematics and science to languages and vocational skills.

The 1980s and 1990s witnessed the proliferation of personal computers, making educational software more accessible. This era saw the emergence of educational games and simulations designed to infuse learning with fun and interactivity. Examples include "The Oregon Trail," a historical simulation game, and "Reader Rabbit," focused on early literacy skills.

Intelligent Tutoring Systems (ITS) also came to the fore during this period, utilizing AI techniques to deliver personalized instruction and feedback. The SCHOLAR system, developed in the 1970s, engaged users in interactive dialogues on various subjects. Another notable example is the Cognitive Tutor by Carnegie Learning, which employs cognitive models to guide students through mathematical learning tasks.

The Ascendancy of Machine Learning in Education

The 21st century heralded significant strides in AI and machine learning, profoundly impacting educational technology. Machine learning, a subset of AI, harnesses algorithms and statistical models to enhance computers' task performance through experiential learning.

One of the prominent applications of machine learning in education is adaptive learning technology. Adaptive learning platforms employ machine learning algorithms to analyze student data, such as assessment performance and interactions with learning materials. This data informs the creation of personalized learning paths tailored to each student's needs. DreamBox, an adaptive math program, and Knewton, offering personalized learning paths across various subjects, exemplify this technology in action.

Machine learning also underpins intelligent tutoring systems, leveraging student interaction data to provide real-time feedback and adjust task difficulty based on performance. For instance, Carnegie Learning's MATHia employs machine learning to offer personalized math instruction aligned with students' learning trajectories.

Automated grading and assessment represent another significant application of machine learning. Algorithms can evaluate assignments and essays with high accuracy and efficiency, alleviating educators' workload and providing prompt feedback to students. Gradescope is a notable example, offering AI-driven grading solutions increasingly adopted by educational institutions.

Furthermore, predictive analytics powered by machine learning aid in identifying at-risk students and intervening proactively to prevent academic setbacks. By analyzing data such as attendance and engagement metrics, AI can forecast which students may struggle and suggest timely interventions, thereby enhancing retention rates and fostering student success.

Language learning has also reaped the benefits of machine learning. AI-driven language learning platforms like Duolingo adapt lessons to learners' proficiency levels and styles, offering personalized feedback and progress tracking.

Case Studies

Trailblazers in Educational Technology
Several pioneering projects and companies have significantly influenced the landscape of educational technology, shaping the widespread adoption and ongoing development of AI and digital tools in education.

1. **PLATO (Programmed Logic for Automatic Teaching Operations):** Developed in the early 1960s at the University of Illinois, PLATO was

among the first computer-based education systems. Its graphical displays, touch screens, and time-sharing operating system paved the way for future online learning communities.

2. **Carnegie Learning and the Cognitive Tutor:** Carnegie Learning's Cognitive Tutor software, founded in the 1990s, applies cognitive psychology principles to mathematics education. Its personalized feedback and adaptive learning features have proven effective in improving student achievement.

3. **Khan Academy:** Established in 2008, Khan Academy offers free online resources, including instructional videos and practice exercises, with personalized learning paths driven by data analytics.

4. **DreamBox Learning:** Founded in 2006, DreamBox employs AI and machine learning to deliver personalized math education for K–8 students, fostering deeper understanding and mastery of mathematical concepts.

5. **Coursera:** Founded in 2012, Coursera partners with universities

worldwide to offer online courses and degrees, utilizing AI and data analytics to provide adaptive learning experiences.

6. **Duolingo:** Launched in 2011, Duolingo employs AI and gamification to offer personalized language learning experiences, making language acquisition accessible and engaging.

These case studies underscore the innovative contributions of educational technology pioneers, showcasing how AI and digital tools have enhanced learning outcomes and accessibility worldwide.

Conclusion

The evolution of educational technology from conventional methods to digital classrooms has been marked by significant milestones and innovations. Early educational software laid the groundwork for advanced applications, while the rise of machine learning has revolutionized personalized learning, assessment, and administrative efficiency.

Pioneers such as PLATO, Carnegie Learning, Khan Academy, DreamBox Learning,

Coursera, and Duolingo have demonstrated the transformative potential of AI and digital tools in education. Their innovations have not only improved learning outcomes but have also made education more accessible and engaging for students globally.

As we continue to harness the power of AI in education, it's crucial to balance technological advancements with ethical considerations, ensuring these tools support and enhance the educational experience for all learners. The ongoing evolution of educational technology promises further exciting developments and opportunities for the future of education.

Chapter 3

Personalized learning enhanced by AI

Personalized learning

Personalized learning is an educational method that customizes teaching, speed, and subject matter to suit each student's distinct needs, interests, and capabilities. Unlike traditional uniform instruction, personalized learning acknowledges the individuality of students' learning styles, strengths, and weaknesses, aiming to offer tailored learning experiences.

Central to personalized learning is the principle that learners should have control over their learning journey. This approach emphasizes student-centered instruction, empowering learners to dictate what and how they learn, as well as the pace of their progress. By accommodating diverse learning preferences and abilities, personalized learning strives to optimize student engagement, motivation, and success.

Personalized learning manifests in various forms, including differentiated instruction, adaptive learning, competency-based education, and student-directed learning. Despite differences in execution, these approaches share the common objective of placing students at the forefront of the learning process, empowering them to take charge of their education.

Utilizing AI to Customize Educational Content

Artificial intelligence (AI) plays a pivotal role in facilitating personalized learning on a large scale. AI algorithms sift through extensive data, including student performance, preferences, and interactions with learning materials, to generate insights and suggestions for personalized instruction.

Machine learning stands out as a key AI technique in personalized learning. By discerning patterns in student data, machine learning algorithms identify individual learning needs and preferences, continually refining their recommendations over time with more data, ensuring increasingly accurate and personalized guidance.

Another significant AI technology in personalized learning is natural language processing (NLP), which enables computers to comprehend and generate human language. This capability facilitates the creation of interactive learning experiences, such as chatbots and virtual tutors, capable of engaging students in natural language conversations.

AI-driven adaptive learning platforms leverage machine learning, NLP, and other AI technologies to deliver customized instruction. These platforms gather data on student performance, behavior, and preferences to tailor content, difficulty levels, and pacing to each student's requirements.

Impact on Student Engagement and Performance

AI-driven personalized learning profoundly impacts student engagement and performance by offering tailored learning experiences that resonate with individual needs and interests, thereby significantly enhancing motivation and engagement.

When students perceive their learning experiences as relevant, challenging, and accessible, they are more likely to actively participate in learning and invest in their academic success. Personalized learning allows students to progress at their own pace, mitigating feelings of frustration or boredom commonly encountered in traditional classroom settings.

Research demonstrates that personalized learning leads to enhanced student achievement. A meta-analysis by the RAND Corporation revealed that students in personalized learning environments exhibited greater improvements in math and reading compared to those in traditional classrooms, with particularly notable gains among disadvantaged students.

Beyond academic outcomes, personalized learning also fosters the development of non-cognitive skills like self-regulation, persistence, and confidence. By granting students greater autonomy in their learning, personalized learning cultivates essential skills crucial for success both in academics and beyond.

Challenges and Ethical Considerations

While AI-driven personalized learning offers numerous benefits, it also presents several challenges and ethical considerations that demand attention.

1. **Data Privacy and Security:** Safeguarding the privacy and security of student data is imperative to

prevent unauthorized access or misuse.

2. **Bias and Fairness:** AI algorithms may inadvertently perpetuate biases present in the training data, potentially resulting in unequal learning opportunities based on factors like race, gender, or socioeconomic status.

3. **Lack of Human Connection:** Despite AI's valuable support, maintaining meaningful human connections is essential for students' social and emotional development.

4. **Digital Equity:** Disparities in access to technology and internet connectivity can exacerbate existing educational inequalities, necessitating efforts to ensure universal access.

5. **Overreliance on Technology:** Personalized learning should complement traditional teaching methods, avoiding an overemphasis on technology that could diminish face-to-face interactions vital for effective learning.

Addressing these challenges and ethical considerations demands a comprehensive approach involving policymakers, educators, technology developers, and other stakeholders. Clear guidelines and policies are essential to ensure the responsible use of AI in personalized learning, prioritizing equity, fairness, and student well-being.

Conclusion

AI-driven personalized learning represents a transformative approach to education with the potential to revolutionize student learning and achievement. By harnessing AI algorithms to tailor instruction, content, and pace to individual needs, personalized learning can enhance student engagement, motivation, and success.

However, realizing the full potential of AI-driven personalized learning necessitates addressing various challenges and ethical considerations, including data privacy, bias, digital equity, and the role of human educators. Through the development of clear guidelines and policies, we can leverage technology to create more inclusive, equitable, and effective learning experiences for all students.

Chapter 4

Intelligent Tutoring
Systems

Definition and examples of Intelligence Tutoring Systems

Intelligent Tutoring Systems (ITS) are computer-based educational tools that mimic human tutors by providing personalized instruction and feedback to students. They utilize artificial intelligence (AI) techniques to tailor instruction according to each student's needs and learning styles, enhancing the efficiency and effectiveness of learning. One key aspect of ITS is their capability to model the cognitive processes involved in learning, allowing them to gauge student understanding and offer customized guidance. This personalized approach sets ITS apart from other educational technologies, facilitating more targeted and efficient learning experiences.

Examples of ITS include:

1. **Cognitive Tutor:** A widely used ITS by Carnegie Learning for mathematics education, offering personalized guidance through problem-solving activities.
2. **AutoTutor:** Developed by the University of Memphis, it provides conversational tutoring across

various subjects, utilizing natural language processing (NLP) for interactive instruction.

3. **ALEKS (Assessment and Learning in Knowledge Spaces):** An adaptive learning platform employing AI to assess and instruct students in math, science, and other subjects based on individual progress.

4. **Duolingo:** Primarily a language learning app, Duolingo incorporates intelligent tutoring elements by personalizing lessons based on learners' strengths, weaknesses, and preferences.

These examples showcase the versatility and effectiveness of ITS across different subjects and domains, demonstrating their ability to support student learning effectively.

How AI Tutors Operate

ITS employs various AI techniques to deliver personalized instruction:

1. **Knowledge Modeling:** ITS uses domain-specific models to represent concepts and skills, aiding in assessing student understanding.

2. **Student Modeling:** Maintaining models of each student's knowledge and preferences enables ITS to adapt instruction accordingly.
3. **Problem Solving and Scaffolding:** ITS guides students through problem-solving tasks, adjusting support levels based on performance.
4. **Data Analysis and Machine Learning:** Analyzing student data helps ITS improve predictions and tailor instruction.
5. **Natural Language Processing (NLP):** Some ITS engage students in dialogue using NLP techniques, enhancing interaction.

These AI techniques allow ITS to simulate human tutors, providing tailored learning experiences for students.

Advantages and disadvantages

Benefits of ITS include personalized instruction, immediate feedback, adaptive learning, scaffolding, and data-driven insights. However, drawbacks include high development costs, limited subject coverage, dependency on technology, a lack of human interaction, and potential bias.

Future Trends in Intelligent Tutoring

ITS may integrate multimodal interaction, enhance NLP capabilities, leverage personalized learning analytics, support collaborative environments, and address ethical and equity considerations to ensure accessibility and inclusivity.

Conclusion

ITS has the potential to transform education by offering personalized and effective instruction through AI and advanced technologies, paving the way for a more equitable education system.

Chapter 5

The Role of Artificial Intelligence in Assessment and Evaluation

Automated Grading System

Artificial intelligence (AI) has brought about a transformative shift in the assessment landscape within education, particularly through the advent of automated grading systems. These systems, powered by AI algorithms, have fundamentally altered how educators evaluate student responses across assignments, quizzes, and exams. They offer a swift and impartial assessment mechanism, providing timely feedback to both students and educators alike.

A significant advantage of automated grading systems lies in their efficiency. Unlike traditional manual grading methods, which are often time-consuming and laborious, automated systems can swiftly process large volumes of assessments, thereby freeing up educators to concentrate on other facets of teaching. Additionally, they ensure students receive prompt feedback on their work, aiding in their learning journey.

Automated grading systems employ various techniques to assess student responses comprehensively.

1. **Utilization of Natural Language Processing (NLP):** NLP algorithms scrutinize written responses to various assignments, detecting grammatical and spelling errors, assessing the coherence and clarity of writing, and gauging the depth of content comprehension.
2. **Integration of Machine Learning:** Machine learning algorithms are trained on extensive datasets of student responses, enabling them to discern patterns and trends in correct and incorrect answers. This knowledge is then applied to grade new submissions automatically, pinpointing common errors and offering targeted feedback.
3. **Harnessing Data Analytics:** These systems gather data on student performance over time, empowering educators to track progress and pinpoint areas for enhancement. Analytics tools generate reports and visual representations, aiding educators in deciphering assessment data and making informed instructional decisions.

The adoption of automated grading systems extends across both conventional classroom setups and online learning platforms. Platforms like Gradescope, Turnitin, and EssayBot exemplify the proliferation of AI-driven grading solutions, increasingly embraced by educational institutions worldwide.

AI's Impact on Formative and Summative Assessments

AI technologies are reshaping both formative and summative assessments within education. Formative assessments, designed to monitor student learning progression and furnish ongoing feedback, witness AI tools providing immediate feedback to students, enabling them to identify strengths and weaknesses and tailor their learning strategies accordingly. For instance, adaptive learning platforms leverage AI algorithms to customize practice activities based on individual student needs, reinforcing key concepts and skills effectively.

In the realm of summative assessments, AI technologies streamline the grading process, augmenting the validity and reliability of assessments. Automated grading systems proficiently evaluate various question formats, including multiple-choice, short-answer, and essay questions, ensuring fairness and objectivity irrespective of individual grader biases or subjectivity.

Moreover, AI facilitates the analysis of assessment data, identifying patterns and trends in student performance. Predictive analytics algorithms forecast student success on forthcoming assessments, aiding educators in the early identification of at-risk students and the provision of targeted support.

Navigating Bias and Fairness in AI-Driven Evaluations

Despite the myriad benefits AI-driven evaluations offer, they pose significant ethical considerations concerning bias and fairness. AI algorithms, trained on historical data, may inadvertently perpetuate biases related to race, gender, socioeconomic status, and other factors. Addressing these biases necessitates meticulous attention to diverse and representative datasets during the training phase.

Transparency and accountability are paramount in AI-driven evaluations. Ensuring stakeholders comprehend the decision-making process behind automated grading systems is imperative for interpretation and challenge of results. Developers must prioritize transparency, elucidating algorithmic functionalities and decision-making processes.

To counter these challenges, researchers and developers are exploring several strategies:

1. **Fairness-aware AI Techniques:** Innovations like fairness-aware machine learning and algorithmic auditing mitigate bias, ensuring equitable outcomes in automated grading systems.
2. **Ethical Guidelines and Standards:** Educational institutions and professional bodies are formulating ethical guidelines to uphold fairness, transparency, and accountability in AI-driven evaluations.
3. **Human Oversight and Review:** Human intervention complements automated grading systems, ensuring fairness and accuracy in decision-making processes.
4. **Continuous Research and Evaluation:** Ongoing research and evaluation of AI-driven evaluation

systems are crucial for identifying and rectifying biases, ensuring the validity and reliability of outcomes.

Case Studies: Implementations and Outcomes

Several case studies shed light on the implementation and ramifications of AI-driven assessment and evaluation systems in education:

1. **Gradescope:** This AI-driven grading platform streamlines the grading process, enhancing consistency and efficiency while preserving accuracy and reliability.
2. **Turnitin:** Employing AI algorithms, Turnitin effectively deters plagiarism and promotes academic integrity when integrated with educational interventions and support services.
3. **EssayBot:** Although EssayBot aids students in generating essays and providing feedback on grammar and style, educators must be mindful of its limitations and emphasize fostering critical thinking and writing skills.

These case studies underscore the diverse applications of AI in assessment and evaluation in education, spotlighting both the benefits and challenges of AI-driven technologies.

Conclusion

AI-driven assessment and evaluation systems offer myriad advantages, including efficiency, objectivity, and scalability. They streamline the grading process, furnish educators with prompt feedback, and augment the validity and reliability of assessments. Nevertheless, ethical considerations regarding bias, fairness, and transparency loom large.

Collaborative efforts between developers and educators are essential to address these challenges and ensure AI-driven assessments yield accurate, reliable, and equitable outcomes. By prioritizing fairness, transparency, and accountability, stakeholders can harness AI's potential to enhance assessment and evaluation practices, fostering student learning and success.

Chapter 6

Artificial Intelligence Enhancing Administrative Efficiency in Educational Institutions

Streamlining Administrative Tasks with the Power of Artificial Intelligence

Within the realm of educational institutions, a multitude of administrative tasks are indispensable for their seamless operation. These tasks span from scheduling classes and managing enrollments to resource allocation and maintenance of student records. Traditionally, the execution of these tasks has been marked by their time-consuming and labor-intensive nature, demanding significant manual effort from administrators and staff.

Artificial Intelligence (AI) presents a promising avenue to streamline administrative tasks in educational institutions. Leveraging AI technologies such as machine learning, natural language processing, and data analytics, these institutions can automate routine processes, optimize resource allocation, and glean valuable insights to bolster decision-making.

One particularly notable area where AI has demonstrated considerable progress is in scheduling. Scheduling classes, exams, and other events can pose significant challenges, especially in large educational institutions characterized by diverse student populations and a plethora of program offerings. AI-powered scheduling systems are capable of analyzing various factors including course requirements, student preferences, and room availability to generate optimal schedules aimed at minimizing conflicts and maximizing efficiency.

Enrollment management stands as another focal point where AI can streamline administrative processes. AI algorithms can sift through historical enrollment data, demographic trends, and other pertinent factors to forecast future enrollment patterns and refine recruitment and retention strategies. AI-driven enrollment management systems can flag at-risk students, suggest targeted interventions, and monitor progress towards enrollment objectives.

Additionally, resource management within educational institutions presents a ripe opportunity for AI optimization. AI algorithms can scrutinize usage patterns, demand forecasts, and budget constraints to fine-tune the allocation of resources such as classrooms, equipment, and personnel. Through dynamically adjusting resource allocations based on evolving needs and priorities, AI can ensure that educational institutions operate with heightened efficiency and efficacy.

Illustrative Examples: Scheduling, Enrollment, and Resource Management

1. **Scheduling**: AI-powered scheduling systems like Ad Astra and CollegeNET utilize machine learning algorithms to craft optimized class schedules, minimizing conflicts and maximizing resource utilization. These systems take into account factors such as course prerequisites, faculty availability, room capacity, and student preferences to craft schedules that cater to the needs of both students and instructors.

2. **Enrollment Management**: AI-driven enrollment management systems, exemplified by platforms like TargetX and Salesforce Education Cloud, sift through historical enrollment data, demographic trends, and student engagement metrics to predict future enrollment patterns and refine recruitment and retention strategies. These systems can flag at-risk students, recommend personalized interventions, and offer real-time

tracking of progress towards enrollment goals.

3. **Resource Management**: AI algorithms can optimize the allocation of resources in educational institutions by analyzing usage patterns, demand forecasts, and budget constraints. For instance, AI-powered scheduling systems can dynamically adjust class schedules and room assignments based on evolving needs and priorities, while AI-driven budgeting tools can propose cost-saving measures and unearth opportunities for efficiency enhancements.

Impact on Educational Institutions

The adoption of AI for administrative efficiency heralds a transformative era for educational institutions, yielding several tangible benefits:

1. **Cost Savings**: By automating routine processes and optimizing resource allocation, AI can curtail administrative overhead and operational costs. This affords educational institutions the opportunity to redirect resources

towards strategic initiatives and student support services, thereby elevating the overall quality of education.

2. **Improved Efficiency**: AI-driven systems streamline administrative tasks, mitigate manual errors, and expedite decision-making processes. This liberates administrators and staff to channel their time and efforts towards higher-value activities such as student engagement, academic advising, and program development.

3. **Enhanced Student Experience**: AI-powered systems have the potential to enrich the student experience by offering more personalized and responsive services. For instance, AI-driven chatbots can address common student queries such as course registration and financial aid in real-time, thereby reducing wait times and fostering higher satisfaction levels.

4. **Data-Driven Decision-Making**: AI generates invaluable insights from data that can inform strategic decision-making and enhance institutional effectiveness. By analyzing enrollment trends, student performance metrics, and resource utilization patterns, educational

institutions can pinpoint opportunities for enhancement and implement evidence-based interventions.

5. **Scalability and Flexibility**: AI-driven systems boast scalability and adaptability, seamlessly accommodating the evolving needs and priorities of educational institutions. As enrollments surge, programs expand, and resource requisites evolve, AI can dynamically adjust to these changes, ensuring that administrative processes remain nimble and effective.

Cost-Benefit Analysis

While the adoption of AI for administrative efficiency promises a plethora of benefits, it also necessitates a careful evaluation of costs and considerations by educational institutions:

1. **Initial Investment**: Implementing AI-powered systems entails an initial investment in technology infrastructure, software licenses, and staff training. Educational institutions must meticulously assess upfront costs and potential return on

investment (ROI) to ascertain the feasibility and value proposition of AI adoption.

2. **Integration Challenges**: Integrating AI systems with existing administrative systems and workflows can be intricate and time-consuming. Educational institutions must meticulously plan and execute the integration process to minimize disruptions and ensure a seamless transition.

3. **Data Privacy and Security**: AI systems hinge on access to extensive volumes of data, encompassing student records, enrollment information, and financial data. Educational institutions must erect robust data privacy and security measures to safeguard sensitive information and comply with regulatory mandates.

4. **Ethical and Equity Considerations**: AI algorithms run the risk of inadvertently perpetuating biases present in the data they are trained on, potentially resulting in unfair or discriminatory outcomes. Educational institutions must accord precedence to fairness, transparency, and accountability in AI-driven

decision-making to ensure equitable treatment for all students.

5. **Maintenance and Support**: AI systems necessitate ongoing maintenance, updates, and technical support to sustain optimal performance and reliability. Educational institutions must earmark resources for these ongoing costs and allocate them judiciously to sustain long-term AI adoption.

A comprehensive cost-benefit analysis can empower educational institutions to gauge the potential risks and rewards of AI adoption for administrative efficiency, enabling them to make informed decisions that align with their strategic objectives and priorities.

Conclusion

Artificial Intelligence represents a formidable toolset to streamline administrative tasks, optimize resource allocation, and augment operational efficiency in educational institutions. By automating routine processes, extracting valuable insights from data, and enriching decision-making capabilities, AI-driven systems hold the promise of transforming administrative operations and enhancing the overall quality of education.

However, the adoption of AI for administrative efficiency necessitates a nuanced understanding of associated costs and considerations by educational institutions. By conducting a thorough cost-benefit analysis, adeptly addressing integration challenges, and foregrounding ethical and equity considerations, educational institutions can harness the full potential of AI adoption while mitigating potential risks.

As AI technologies continue to evolve and mature, educational institutions stand poised to leverage these tools to forge more responsive, efficient, and student-centered administrative processes that bolster student success and institutional excellence.

Chapter 7

Advancing Special Education Through AI

Introduction

Special education, integral to inclusive education, endeavors to meet the distinctive requirements of students with disabilities, ensuring equitable access to learning opportunities. Nevertheless, tailoring support and instruction to diverse learning needs poses challenges for educators. Artificial intelligence (AI) offers innovative avenues to enhance special education, furnishing customized interventions, facilitating varied instruction, and fostering improved outcomes for students with disabilities.

AI Tools for Tailored Instruction

Differentiated instruction, acknowledging and catering to diverse learning needs, interests, and capabilities, can be bolstered by AI tools, delivering personalized learning experiences tailored to individual preferences and needs.

1. **Adaptive Learning Platforms:** These platforms, driven by AI algorithms, scrutinize student performance data to pinpoint learning gaps, delivering focused instruction and practice activities. They

dynamically adjust instruction difficulty and pace based on student responses, offering appropriate support and challenges.

2. **Personalized Tutoring Systems:** AI-driven tutoring systems like Carnegie Learning's Cognitive Tutor and Knewton's Adaptive Learning Platform deliver personalized instruction and feedback. Utilizing machine learning, they model student knowledge and skills, tailoring instruction and tracking progress.

3. **Natural Language Processing (NLP) Tools:** NLP tools aid students with disabilities such as dyslexia or speech impairments by furnishing alternative communication modes. For instance, speech-to-text and text-to-speech technologies assist dyslexic students in accessing written materials, while voice recognition aids those with speech impairments in verbal expression.

4. **Virtual Reality (VR) and Augmented Reality (AR) Applications:** VR and AR technologies offer immersive, interactive learning experiences, engaging students with disabilities and facilitating experiential learning.

VR simulations provide practical training in real-world scenarios like vocational training, while AR overlays digital content onto physical environments, enriching learning and engagement.

Supporting Students with Disabilities

AI holds promise in revolutionizing support and services for students with disabilities, fostering inclusive, equitable educational opportunities.

1. **Personalized Learning Plans:** AI tools aid educators in devising personalized learning plans, accommodating individual strengths, needs, and goals. These plans delineate specific accommodations, modifications, and interventions.
2. **Accessibility Features:** AI enhances accessibility in educational materials and technologies, rendering them more usable for students with disabilities. Screen readers, magnification tools, and voice commands assist visually impaired students, while alternative input

methods aid those with motor impairments.

3. **Data-Driven Interventions:** AI analytics scrutinize student performance data, identifying learning and behavioral patterns for early intervention. Predictive analytics forecast academic success likelihood or dropout risk, enabling preventive measures.

4. **Assistive Technologies:** AI-powered assistive technologies like speech recognition and predictive text input aid students in accessing and producing written content, overcoming barriers to reading, writing, and communication.

Case Studies Success Stories and Best Practices

Several case studies illustrate successful AI implementation in special education, supporting students with disabilities:

1. **The Reading Assistant:** Scientific Learning Corporation's AI-driven literacy program, The Reading Assistant, aids students with reading difficulties, including dyslexia,

offering individualized instruction and feedback.

2. **Brain Power:** This company develops AI-powered social-emotional learning and communication tools for individuals with autism spectrum disorder (ASD), showing improvements in social communication and self-regulation.

3. **Google's Lookout:** An AI-powered accessibility app, Lookout assists visually impaired individuals in navigating the physical environment independently.

Future Prospects and Innovations

The future of AI in special education holds promise for innovation:

1. **Personalized Learning Environments:** Evolving AI technologies will offer more personalized and adaptive learning experiences, tailored to individual preferences and needs.

2. **Augmented Reality (AR) and Virtual Reality (VR):** These technologies will play a pivotal role,

providing immersive, interactive learning experiences.
3. Natural Language Processing (NLP) and Speech Recognition: NLP and speech recognition technologies will enable more natural communication and interaction for students with disabilities.
4. Data Analytics and Predictive Modeling: Advanced AI analytics will offer educators actionable insights into student learning and behavior.

Conclusion

AI presents vast potential to enhance special education, fostering improved outcomes for students with disabilities. Collaboration among educators, policymakers, and technology developers is crucial to ensure equitable, accessible AI-driven solutions, empowering students with disabilities to succeed academically, socially, and personally, and fostering a more inclusive learning environment for all.

Chapter 8

Language Acquisition and AI Introduction

Introduction

Language acquisition is pivotal in education, enabling individuals to effectively communicate and interact with their surroundings. Artificial Intelligence (AI) has emerged as a potent instrument in enhancing language education, offering innovative solutions to aid learners in acquiring new languages, refining language skills, and overcoming communication barriers. This chapter delves into the manifold applications of AI in language education, encompassing translation tools, language tutoring systems, and the broader impact of AI on global education.

AI Applications in Language Education

1. **Automated Language Evaluation:** AI-driven assessment tools scrutinize learners' oral and written responses to gauge their language proficiency. These tools furnish instant feedback on grammar, vocabulary, pronunciation, and fluency, assisting learners in identifying areas for enhancement and monitoring their progress.

2. **Personalized Language Learning Platforms:** AI-powered platforms for language learning employ adaptive algorithms to customize instruction according to individual learners' requirements and preferences. These platforms analyze learners' performance data to pinpoint strengths and weaknesses, tailor instructional content and activities, and furnish focused practice and feedback.

3. **Language Translation and Interpretation:** AI-based translation tools, exemplified by Google Translate and DeepL, utilize neural machine translation algorithms to interpret text and speech across different languages. These tools facilitate communication and information exchange, enabling learners to access content in multiple languages and engage with diverse linguistic communities.

4. **Language Tutoring Systems:** AI-driven tutoring systems for language learning, such as Duolingo and Babbel, offer interactive and personalized instruction through mobile applications and online platforms. These systems utilize

natural language processing (NLP) techniques to engage learners in dialogue, assess their language skills, and deliver real-time feedback and guidance.

Translation Tools and Language Tutors

1. **Google Translate:** Among the most widely utilized AI-driven translation tools, Google Translate provides translation services for text, speech, and images in over 100 languages. Employing neural machine translation algorithms, Google Translate furnishes accurate and natural-sounding translations, facilitating communication and information access across language barriers.

2. **Duolingo:** Duolingo, a prominent AI-driven language learning platform, offers courses in over 30 languages. Leveraging gamification techniques, spaced repetition algorithms, and personalized learning paths, Duolingo encourages active participation in language learning. The platform provides interactive

lessons, quizzes, and practice activities covering vocabulary, grammar, listening, speaking, and reading skills.

3. **DeepL:** DeepL, an AI-powered translation tool, employs deep learning algorithms to generate high-quality translations with enhanced accuracy and fluency compared to traditional machine translation systems. DeepL offers translation services for text and documents in multiple languages, catering to the needs of businesses, researchers, and individuals requiring dependable translation solutions.

4. **Babbel:** Babbel, an AI-driven language tutoring platform, delivers courses in 14 languages. Emphasizing conversational proficiency and practical language skills, Babbel provides interactive lessons, dialogues, and exercises covering vocabulary, grammar, pronunciation, and cultural context. The platform utilizes speech recognition technology to assess learners' pronunciation and furnish feedback for improvement.

Impact on Global Education

1. **Accessibility and Inclusivity:** AI-powered language learning tools enhance the accessibility and inclusivity of language education by offering flexible and cost-effective learning opportunities globally. These tools mitigate barriers to access such as geographic location, socioeconomic status, and physical disabilities, enabling learners from diverse backgrounds to engage in language learning.

2. **Cultural Exchange and Understanding:** AI translation tools facilitate communication and cultural exchange between speakers of different languages, fostering mutual understanding and appreciation of diverse linguistic and cultural heritage. These tools bridge language gaps and encourage cross-cultural collaboration, dialogue, and cooperation in global education and beyond.

3. **Workforce Development:** Language proficiency is a vital skill for global citizenship and workforce readiness in an interconnected world. AI-driven language learning platforms equip

learners with the linguistic and communicative skills necessary for success in various professional domains, including international business, diplomacy, tourism, and academia.

4. **Lifelong Learning:** AI-powered language learning platforms support lifelong learning by offering adaptable and personalized learning experiences that accommodate learners' evolving needs and interests. These platforms enable learners to pursue language learning at their own pace, schedule, and in alignment with their personal and professional objectives throughout their lives.

Challenges and Future Trends

1. **Accuracy and Reliability:** Despite notable advancements, AI translation and language learning tools may encounter challenges in accuracy, fluency, and cultural nuances, particularly in complex or specialized domains. Enhancing the accuracy and reliability of AI algorithms remains a significant challenge for developers and researchers.

2. **Data Privacy and Security:** AI-driven language learning platforms gather and analyze substantial amounts of user data, including personal information and learning metrics. Safeguarding the privacy and security of user data is imperative to maintain trust and compliance with data protection regulations.

3. **Equity and Access:** While AI-powered language learning tools hold promise in democratizing language education, disparities in technology access and internet connectivity may exacerbate existing educational inequalities. Ensuring equitable access to AI-driven language learning opportunities for learners from underserved communities is a critical challenge.

4. **Ethical and Sociocultural Considerations:** AI translation and language learning tools raise ethical and sociocultural concerns related to linguistic diversity, cultural representation, and linguistic imperialism. Developers and educators must navigate these complex issues sensitively to promote linguistic diversity, cultural

sensitivity, and inclusive language education practices.

Conclusion

AI stands poised to revolutionize language education by providing personalized, accessible, and inclusive learning experiences worldwide. From translation tools and language tutors to automated assessment and personalized learning platforms, AI-driven technologies offer innovative solutions to support learners in language acquisition, skill enhancement, and engagement with diverse linguistic communities. As AI continues to evolve, collaboration among educators, policymakers, and technology developers is vital to address challenges, promote ethical practices, and harness AI's full potential in advancing global education and fostering cross-cultural understanding and cooperation. Leveraging the transformative power of AI in language education empowers learners to become effective communicators, critical thinkers, and engaged global citizens in an interconnected world.

Chapter 9

AI's Role in Educational Research

Introduction

Educational research holds significant importance in shaping teaching methods, educational policies, and our comprehension of learning mechanisms. With the integration of artificial intelligence (AI), researchers now possess potent tools for scrutinizing educational data, detecting patterns, and deriving practical insights. This chapter delves into the utilization of AI in educational research, emphasizing its application in data analysis, predictive analytics, trend identification, and ethical considerations concerning data usage.

Utilizing AI for Educational Data Analysis

1. **Data Collection and Management:** AI technologies streamline the gathering, storage, and administration of educational data from diverse sources like student records, assessments, and online platforms. AI-powered systems efficiently handle vast data volumes, ensuring data quality, integrity, and automating mundane data processing tasks.

2. **Data Preprocessing and Cleaning:** AI algorithms prepare educational data for analysis by standardizing, detecting anomalies, filling missing values, and refining features. These AI-driven tools simplify data preparation, saving researchers time and enhancing analysis quality.

3. **Data Analysis and Modeling:** Machine learning and data mining empower researchers to dissect educational data, unveiling hidden patterns, relationships, and future trends. These techniques identify factors impacting student learning outcomes and predict forthcoming educational trends and challenges. Predictive Analytics in Education

4. **Student Performance Prediction:** Predictive analytics forecast student performance based on historical data and demographic factors, aiding in identifying students needing additional support for academic success.

5. **Retention and Dropout Prediction:** Predictive models recognize students at risk of dropping out, enabling timely interventions to enhance retention and support student success.

6. **Course and Program Evaluation:** Predictive analytics evaluate educational programs and interventions by analyzing student performance data, guiding improvements to boost learning outcomes and program quality. AI for Identifying Trends and Patterns

7. **Learning Analytics:** AI-driven learning analytics unveil student behavior patterns, facilitating personalized instruction and optimizing learning experiences.

8. **Research Synthesis and Meta-Analysis:** AI tools synthesize educational research literature, identifying trends and gaps to inform evidence-based decision-making and research priorities.

9. **Social Network Analysis:** AI algorithms analyze social interactions within educational communities, fostering collaboration and knowledge exchange. Ethical Considerations in Data Use

10. **Data Privacy and Confidentiality:** Researchers must safeguard educational data privacy and comply with regulations like FERPA, ensuring secure data handling.

11. **Fairness and Bias:** Researchers must address biases in AI algorithms to prevent unfair outcomes and ensure equitable treatment.
12. **Informed Consent and Data Ownership:** Obtaining informed consent from participants and clarifying data ownership rights uphold transparency and accountability. Conclusion AI offers transformative potential in educational research by enabling comprehensive data analysis, trend prediction, and actionable insights. However, researchers must navigate ethical concerns surrounding data privacy, fairness, and transparency responsibly to uphold principles of equity and respect for human rights. By embracing AI responsibly, researchers can contribute to educational advancement, benefiting learners, educators, and society.

Chapter 10

The Fusion of Gamification and Artificial Intelligence in Educational Settings

Introduction

In recent years, the integration of gaming elements and mechanics into non-game environments, known as gamification, has garnered significant attention in educational circles. This approach aims to captivate learners, boost motivation, and enhance learning outcomes. The emergence of artificial intelligence (AI) has propelled gamification in education even further, offering opportunities to create more adaptive, personalized, and immersive learning experiences. This chapter delves into the convergence of gamification and AI within education, exploring AI's role in educational games, successful instances of gamified learning platforms through case studies, the advantages and constraints of gamification, and potential future trajectories in this burgeoning field.

The Role of AI in Educational Games

1. **Adaptive Learning:** AI algorithms are instrumental in scrutinizing learners' performance data within educational games, enabling adjustments in difficulty levels,

pacing, and content to cater to individual learning requisites and preferences. Adaptive learning systems employ machine learning methodologies to model learners' competencies, skills, and learning paths, thereby furnishing personalized guidance and feedback in real-time.

2. **Intelligent Tutoring Systems (ITS):** Educational games embedded with AI-powered intelligent tutoring systems offer tailored instruction, guidance, and assistance to learners. Leveraging natural language processing (NLP), these systems engage learners in dialogue, evaluate comprehension levels, and furnish targeted feedback and hints to scaffold learning processes.

3. **Emotion Recognition and Feedback:** AI technologies such as affective computing and emotion recognition can discern learners' emotional states and engagement levels during gameplay by analyzing facial expressions, gestures, and physiological signals. This insight enables educational games to deliver adaptive feedback, interventions, and

support to regulate learners' emotions and sustain motivation levels.

Case Studies: Exemplary Gamified Learning Platforms

1. **Kahoot!:** Renowned for its game-based quizzes, challenges, and competitions, Kahoot! stands as a prominent gamified learning platform spanning various subjects and topics. The platform harnesses AI algorithms to scrutinize learners' responses, monitor progress, and formulate personalized recommendations for further practice and review.

2. **Classcraft:** Serving as a gamified classroom management platform, Classcraft employs game mechanics such as avatars, quests, and rewards to incentivize students and foster positive behavior. AI-powered analytics integrated into the platform track students' engagement, collaboration, and academic performance, empowering educators to deliver targeted interventions and support.

3. **Prodigy:** Prodigy offers an immersive math learning platform

that gamifies math practice and skill development. By leveraging AI algorithms, the platform customizes the difficulty level and pacing of math problems based on individual student performance, ensuring tailored learning experiences for each learner.

Advantages and Constraints

1. **Advantages of AI-driven Gamification:**

   - Enhanced Engagement and Motivation: Gamification enriches learner engagement and motivation by infusing learning activities with elements of enjoyment, interactivity, and gratification.
   - **Personalized Learning:** AI-driven gamification facilitates personalized learning experiences that adapt dynamically to individual learning needs, preferences, and progress.
   - **Real-time Feedback and Progress Tracking:**

Educational games integrated with AI analytics furnish real-time feedback and progress tracking, enabling learners to monitor their performance and chart their learning trajectories.

- **Skill Development:** Gamification nurtures the cultivation of critical thinking, problem-solving abilities, collaboration, and other essential 21st-century skills imperative for success in the digital era.

2. **Constraints and Challenges:**

- **Complexity in Implementation:** Designing and implementing AI-infused gamified learning experiences entails complexity and resource intensiveness, necessitating proficiency in game design, AI algorithms, and educational pedagogy.
- Overemphasis on External Rewards: Gamification risks accentuating reliance on extrinsic rewards such as

points, badges, and leaderboards, potentially undermining intrinsic motivation and authentic learning experiences.

- Equity and Accessibility Concerns: Gamified learning platforms featuring AI analytics may exacerbate existing discrepancies in technology access and internet connectivity, thereby disadvantaging learners from underserved communities.

- Ethical Considerations: The utilization of AI in gamification gives rise to ethical considerations concerning data privacy, fairness, and transparency, mandating concerted efforts to ensure responsible and ethical utilization of educational technologies.

Future Trajectories

1. **AI-driven Personalization:** Future iterations of gamified learning platforms will harness AI

technologies to offer heightened levels of adaptability, personalization, and responsiveness in learning experiences tailored to individual learner requisites and preferences.

2. **Immersive and Interactive Experiences:** Advancements in virtual reality (VR), augmented reality (AR), and mixed reality (MR) technologies will unlock new vistas for immersive and interactive gamified learning encounters that engage multiple senses and foster deeper levels of learning engagement.

3. **Collaborative and Social Learning:** AI-powered gamification will facilitate collaborative and social learning encounters, empowering learners to collaborate, communicate, and co-create knowledge with peers in virtual realms.

4. **Ethical and Inclusive Design:** Future iterations of gamified learning platforms will prioritize ethical and inclusive design tenets, ensuring that AI-driven gamification promotes equity, diversity, accessibility, and learner well-being.

Conclusion

The fusion of gamification with AI harbors the potential to revolutionize education by furnishing engaging, personalized, and efficacious learning experiences for learners spanning diverse age cohorts and backgrounds. From adaptive learning frameworks and intelligent tutoring systems to immersive virtual environments and collaborative social learning engagements, the amalgamation of gamification and AI presents a panorama of thrilling possibilities for innovation and progression in education. Nonetheless, to harness the full potential of AI-infused gamification, stakeholders including educators, researchers, policymakers, and technology developers must collaborate diligently to tackle challenges, espouse best practices, and uphold ethical and inclusive design principles. By harnessing the transformative synergy of gamification and AI in education, we can empower learners to evolve into active, engaged, and lifelong learner's adept at navigating the complexities of the digital epoch.

Chapter 11

The Fusion of Virtual and Augmented Reality Empowered by Artificial Intelligence

Introduction

Virtual Reality (VR) and Augmented Reality (AR) have emerged as formidable tools in crafting immersive and interactive educational experiences. When coupled with Artificial Intelligence (AI), the amalgamation of VR and AR offers tailored, adaptable, and captivating learning environments that amplify educational outcomes and student engagement. This chapter delves into the synergy between VR/AR and AI for immersive learning, illustrating instances of their application in education, evaluating their impact on learning achievements, and scrutinizing the challenges and prospects they present.

Integrating VR/AR with AI for Immersive Learning

1. **Tailored Learning Environments:** AI algorithms meticulously scrutinize learner data and preferences, tailoring VR/AR experiences to suit individual learning requisites and preferences. Adaptive learning systems adeptly tweak the content, pacing, and complexity of VR/AR simulations,

optimizing learning outcomes for each learner.

2. **Intelligent Tutoring Systems:** AI-infused intelligent tutoring systems integrated into VR/AR applications furnish real-time feedback, guidance, and assistance to learners. Leveraging Natural Language Processing (NLP) and machine learning algorithms, these systems engage learners in dialogues, assess their comprehension, and dispense personalized instruction and aid.

3. **Emotion Recognition and Feedback:** AI innovations such as affective computing and emotion recognition discern learners' facial expressions, gestures, and physiological cues, gauging their emotional disposition and engagement levels during VR/AR experiences. This feedback enables VR/AR applications to tailor content and interactions, perpetuating learner motivation and engagement.

Examples of VR/AR in Education

1. **Virtual Laboratories:** VR simulations empower students to conduct experiments and delve into

scientific concepts within virtual laboratory settings. Platforms like Labster and zSpace proffer immersive VR encounters mirroring real-world lab setups, enabling students to practice lab techniques and procedures safely and economically.

2. **Augmented Reality Textbooks:** AR-augmented textbooks overlay digital content, including interactive 3D models, animations, and multimedia, onto printed textbooks. Platforms like Curiscope and QuiverVision exploit AR technology to animate educational content, fostering a more engaging and interactive learning milieu for students.

3. **Virtual Field Trips:** VR field trips transport students to remote locales, historical landmarks, and cultural sites virtually. Applications like Google Expeditions and Nearpod VR empower educators to orchestrate immersive virtual excursions, delivering rich, experiential learning experiences that deepen comprehension and retention of subject matter.

Impact on Learning Outcomes

1. **Enhanced Engagement:** VR/AR experiences ensnare students' attention and kindle their curiosity, resulting in heightened levels of engagement and motivation to learn. The immersive nature of VR/AR environments nurtures active exploration and participation, engendering profound learning experiences.

2. **Amplified Retention and Recall:** VR/AR simulations furnish multisensory experiences conducive to experiential learning, augmenting retention of information. Studies evince that learners retain more knowledge and recollect information more effectively when immersed in VR/AR environments compared to conventional methodologies.

3. **Improved Spatial Comprehension:** VR/AR technologies bolster spatial cognition and spatial reasoning skills by enabling students to interact with three-dimensional objects and environments. This spatial acumen is particularly advantageous in disciplines such as mathematics, engineering, and architecture,

wherein visualization holds paramount significance.

Challenges and Opportunities

1. **Cost and Accessibility:** The exorbitant cost of VR/AR hardware and software, coupled with the requisite technical expertise, may impede adoption and accessibility for certain educational institutions and learners. Nonetheless, technological advancements and the proliferation of affordable VR/AR devices proffer opportunities to surmount these challenges and broaden access to immersive learning experiences.
2. **Content Creation and Curation:** Crafting high-quality VR/AR content necessitates proficiency in instructional design, content creation, and software development. Educators and instructional designers necessitate support and resources to fashion and curate immersive learning experiences aligned with educational objectives and standards.
3. **Ethical and Social Ramifications:** VR/AR technologies beckon ethical and social considerations pertaining to privacy, safety, and digital

citizenship. Educators must address these concerns and advocate responsible utilization of VR/AR in education to safeguard learners' rights and well-being.

4. **Integration with Curriculum and Pedagogy:** Seamless integration of VR/AR into educational praxis mandates alignment with curriculum objectives, instructional methodologies, and pedagogical paradigms. Educators necessitate training and professional development opportunities to effectively harness VR/AR technologies in bolstering teaching and learning.

Conclusion

The fusion of virtual and augmented reality with artificial intelligence harbors immense potential for revolutionizing education by engendering immersive, personalized, and engaging learning experiences. From tailored learning environments and intelligent tutoring systems to virtual laboratories and augmented reality textbooks, VR/AR fortified by AI offers innovative solutions to enhance learning outcomes and student engagement. Nonetheless, realizing the full potential of VR/AR in education necessitates addressing challenges pertaining to cost, accessibility, content creation, and ethical considerations. By capitalizing on the opportunities afforded by these technologies and collaboratively confronting these challenges, educators, researchers, and policymakers can harness the transformative prowess of VR/AR to forge more inclusive, equitable, and efficacious learning environments for all learners.

Chapter 12

Facilitating Teacher Training and Professional Development

Introduction

In contemporary educational frameworks, the significance of teacher training and continuous professional development cannot be overstated. As technological advancements, notably artificial intelligence (AI), surge forward, there exists a burgeoning opportunity to revolutionize the methodologies employed in the training and sustenance of educators. This chapter delves into the pivotal role of AI within teacher training and ongoing professional development, meticulously examining AI-infused tools designed for teacher training, their consequential impact on the quality of teaching, and prospective trends and innovations poised to redefine this domain.

AI Tools for Teacher Training

1. **Advanced AI-Integrated Learning Management Systems (LMS):** By incorporating AI algorithms into learning management systems, comprehensive evaluations of teacher performance data encompassing assessment scores, lesson plans, and student interactions are rendered feasible. These systems proffer

personalized feedback and recommendations tailored towards ameliorating instructional methodologies, thereby furnishing profound insights into pedagogical strategies.

2. **Immersive Virtual Simulation Environments:** Propelled by AI, virtual simulation environments offer aspiring educators a simulated platform to hone their teaching skills amidst lifelike scenarios, obviating the necessity for physical classrooms or real students. This facilitates the exploration of varied instructional paradigms and classroom management strategies within a secure and controlled milieu.

3. **Intelligent Tutoring Systems (ITS):** Harnessing AI algorithms, ITS deliver tailored instruction and assistance to burgeoning educators, furnishing interactive lessons, quizzes, and practice sessions meticulously crafted to cater to individualized learning requisites. Through such platforms, aspiring teachers can fortify their proficiency and confidence in pedagogical endeavors.

4. **Utilization of Data Analytics and Predictive Modeling:** AI-driven analytics tools adeptly scrutinize voluminous educational data to discern patterns, trends, and areas necessitating refinement within teacher training programs. Predictive modeling algorithms prognosticate teacher performance and retention, thereby enabling institutions to preemptively address challenges and foster professional growth.

Ongoing Professional Development with AI

1. **Tailored Learning Trajectories:** AI-driven professional development platforms curate personalized learning pathways contingent upon educators' interests, aspirations, and learning proclivities. These platforms employ adaptive algorithms to recommend pertinent resources, courses, and activities meticulously aligned with the professional developmental needs of educators.

2. **Microlearning and Incremental Learning Modules:** AI-infused microlearning platforms dispense

succinct, targeted learning modules and resources that can be accessed ubiquitously. Such bite-sized learning experiences facilitate the incremental acquisition of knowledge and skills, accommodating professional development within the constraints of educators' busy schedules.

3. **Collaborative Learning Communities:** AI fosters collaborative endeavors and knowledge dissemination amongst educators via online communities, social networking platforms, and professional learning networks. These virtual enclaves serve as conduits for peer-to-peer interaction, thereby facilitating the exchange of best practices and collaborative problem-solving initiatives.

4. **Feedback Mechanisms and Reflexive Tools:** AI-driven feedback mechanisms and reflexive tools empower educators to solicit feedback on their pedagogical endeavors and engage in reflective practices conducive to professional growth. Leveraging natural language processing (NLP) techniques, these tools analyze written reflections, peer feedback, and classroom

observations, thereby furnishing actionable insights for enhancement.

Impact on Teaching Quality

1. **Augmented Pedagogical Acumen and Proficiency:** AI-infused teacher training initiatives augment educators' comprehension of pedagogical concepts, instructional methodologies, and technological integrations. By assimilating AI into their teaching repertoire, educators can augment their efficacy and precipitate enhanced student learning outcomes.

2. **Refined Differentiation and Personalization:** AI enables educators to tailor instruction and personalize learning experiences, thereby catering to the diverse needs of their students adeptly. By harnessing AI tools and analytics, educators can adapt teaching modalities, curricula, and assessments to accommodate individual learning predilections, proclivities, and aptitudes.

3. **Elevated Efficiency and Efficacy:** AI expedites administrative undertakings, such as curriculum

development, grading, and assessment, thereby affording educators ample time to concentrate on instructional planning and student engagement. By automating routine tasks and furnishing actionable insights, AI engenders heightened teaching efficiency and efficacy.

4. **Cultivation of a Culture of Continuous Improvement:** AI instills a culture of perpetual refinement within the realms of teaching and learning by furnishing educators with ongoing feedback, support, and resources for professional development. By embracing AI-driven innovations, educators remain abreast of emerging educational paradigms, research findings, and pedagogical best practices.

Future Trends and Innovations

1. **AI-Powered Mentorship and Coaching Initiatives:** Future professional development endeavors may encompass AI-powered mentorship and coaching systems, which furnish personalized guidance and support to educators. These

virtual mentors proffer tailored feedback, recommendations, and resources meticulously aligned with individualized educator requisites and aspirations.

2. **Immersive Learning Environments:** AI-facilitated virtual and augmented reality technologies are slated to engender immersive learning environments tailored for teacher training and professional development. Such environments afford educators the opportunity to simulate teaching scenarios, receive feedback from virtual entities, and engage in collaborative endeavors within virtual classrooms.

3. **Integration of Natural Language Processing (NLP) Assistants:** AI-driven NLP assistants are poised to support educators in myriad capacities, ranging from lesson planning to student interaction facilitation. These virtual assistants are adept at generating personalized recommendations, addressing queries, and fostering seamless communication and collaboration amongst educators.

4. **Embrace of Data-Driven Decision-Making Paradigms:** AI analytics

tools will furnish educators with the means to make data-driven decisions regarding teacher training and professional development initiatives. By analyzing teacher performance metrics, student outcomes, and program efficacy, institutions can delineate areas necessitating enhancement and allocate resources judiciously.

Conclusion

AI stands as a potent catalyst poised to metamorphose teacher training and professional development paradigms by furnishing educators with personalized, adaptive, and immersive learning experiences. From AI-driven learning management systems and virtual simulation environments to bespoke professional development platforms and data analytics tools, AI proffers innovative solutions aimed at bolstering educator growth and amplifying teaching efficacy.

As AI continues to burgeon and shape the educational landscape, collaboration amongst educators, policymakers, and technology developers is imperative to harness its full potential within the realms of teacher training and professional development. By embracing AI-driven innovations and cultivating a culture of lifelong learning, educators can fortify their teaching efficacy, elevate student learning outcomes, and ultimately, spearhead advancements within the realm of education in the digital epoch.

Chapter 13

Exploring Ethical and Privacy Considerations in the Context of Artificial Intelligence Integration into Education

Introduction

With the pervasive integration of artificial intelligence (AI) into educational settings, heightened attention is being directed towards issues surrounding data privacy, ethical ramifications, and the conscientious deployment of AI technologies. This chapter undertakes an in-depth examination of the ethical and privacy considerations associated with the adoption of AI-driven education. It delves into topics including data privacy challenges, ethical dilemmas stemming from AI utilization, the delicate equilibrium between fostering innovation and upholding responsibility, and the imperative role of policy and regulation in this evolving landscape.

Data Privacy in AI-Driven Education

1. **Student Data Collection and Utilization:** Educational systems powered by AI amass and scrutinize vast troves of student data, encompassing personal details, academic histories, and behavioral trends. In this milieu, concerns naturally emerge regarding the

safeguarding of data privacy, the fortification against unauthorized access or misuse, and the assurance of data security.

2. **Ensuring Informed Consent and Transparent Practices:** Ethical imperatives dictate the necessity of furnishing students, parents, and educators with comprehensive insight into the collection, utilization, and storage modalities of their data within AI-driven educational ecosystems. Transparency in policies and procedures governing data management, coupled with the procurement of informed consent, serves as a cornerstone in upholding privacy rights and engendering trust in these systems.

3. **Empowering Data Ownership and Control:** Paramount to the ethical underpinnings of AI-driven education is the elucidation of rights pertaining to data ownership and the establishment of mechanisms enabling individuals, including students and educators, to exercise control over their data. Facilitating avenues for data access, modification, or deletion, as well as delineating clear protocols governing data

sharing and utilization, is essential for the preservation of individuals' privacy prerogatives.

Ethical Implications of AI Utilization

1. **Mitigating Bias and Ensuring Fairness:** The propensity of AI algorithms to mirror biases entrenched within the data they are trained upon underscores the imperative of proactively addressing algorithmic biases to forestall the propagation of inequitable or discriminatory outcomes. Safeguarding fairness and equity mandates meticulous scrutiny of algorithmic predispositions and the implementation of measures geared towards their amelioration.

2. **Fostering Transparency and Accountability:** Ethical employment of AI mandates the cultivation of transparency and accountability within the sphere of algorithmic decision-making. Stakeholders, including educators and developers, must undertake endeavors to comprehend the operational

mechanics of AI algorithms, evaluate their impact on learners and other stakeholders, and ensure that decisions engendered by AI systems are lucidly explicable and subject to scrutiny.

3. **Upholding Student Well-Being and Autonomy:** The advent of AI-driven educational technologies precipitates apprehensions regarding the well-being and agency of students. There exists a latent peril of excessive reliance on AI systems in decision-making processes, potentially undermining students' autonomy. Ethical imperatives necessitate that AI serves as a supplement rather than a surrogate for human judgment in educational contexts.

Balancing Innovation with Responsibility

1. **Embracing Ethical Design and Development Tenets:** The ethical compass must remain steadfastly oriented towards considerations of fairness, transparency, accountability, and privacy throughout the lifecycle of AI-driven

educational technologies. Prioritizing ethical design principles serves as a lodestar for innovation endeavors in this domain.

2. **Cultivating Educator Proficiency and Awareness:** Equipping educators with the requisite acumen and awareness pertaining to ethical and privacy dimensions in AI-driven education assumes paramount significance. Educators must be adept at discerning the ethical ramifications of AI utilization, identifying potential biases and risks, and making judicious decisions vis-à-vis the integration of AI technologies in pedagogical practices.

3. **Nurturing Stakeholder Engagement and Collaborative Discourse:** Enlisting the active participation of stakeholders spanning students, parents, educators, policymakers, and technology developers in deliberations pertaining to ethical and privacy considerations in AI-driven education engenders collaborative synergies and facilitates consensus-building. The inclusion of stakeholders in decision-making processes serves as a linchpin for

assuaging concerns and instilling confidence in AI technologies.

Policy and Regulation Imperatives

1. **Fortifying Data Protection Regimes:** Policymakers bear the onus of fortifying data protection regimes and enacting robust privacy laws to shield individuals' personal data within the ambit of AI-driven education. Adherence to regulatory frameworks such as the General Data Protection Regulation (GDPR) in Europe and the Family Educational Rights and Privacy Act (FERPA) in the United States constitutes a linchpin in safeguarding students' privacy entitlements.
2. **Crafting Ethical Guidelines and Frameworks:** The formulation of ethical guidelines and frameworks tailored to the nuances of AI-driven education holds promise in furnishing educators, developers, and policymakers with navigational aids. These frameworks ought to encapsulate ethical precepts germane to data privacy, algorithmic bias, transparency, accountability, and student well-being.

3. **Instituting Ethics Oversight Mechanisms:** The establishment of ethics review boards or committees tasked with the evaluation of the ethical ramifications attendant to AI-driven educational initiatives serves as a bulwark against potential risks and ethical lapses. These oversight bodies serve to provide scrutiny, guidance, and ethical appraisal of AI projects, ensuring fidelity to ethical norms and principles.

Conclusion

In navigating the terrain of AI-driven education, ethical and privacy considerations loom large, necessitating astute deliberation and proactive measures. By accordant primacy to tenets such as data privacy, ethical design, transparency, and accountability, stakeholders ranging from educators to policymakers can steer the course towards the responsible and ethical deployment of AI technologies in education. Striking a harmonious balance between innovation and responsibility entails the fostering of stakeholder engagement, the augmentation of educator proficiency and awareness, and the institution of policies and regulations geared towards upholding individuals' privacy rights and ethical imperatives. Through concerted collaborative endeavors aimed at addressing ethical and privacy concerns, the transformative potential of AI in education can be harnessed while safeguarding the rights and well-being of learners and stakeholders alike.

Chapter 14

Exploring Case Studies and Real-World Applications in Education

Introduction

The investigation into real-world case studies serves as a valuable tool for understanding the practical application of artificial intelligence (AI) across diverse educational landscapes. This chapter delves into comprehensive case studies showcasing AI integration in education, shedding light on successful implementations, valuable lessons learned, encountered challenges, and the promising future prospects.

Case Study 1: Adoption of Adaptive Learning Platforms

Description: Adaptive learning platforms leverage AI algorithms to tailor instruction and content delivery to suit individual student requirements and learning preferences.

Success Story: Within a K-12 school district, the adoption of an adaptive learning platform facilitated personalized learning experiences in mathematics. Through the analysis of student performance data and targeted interventions, the platform yielded positive outcomes, including heightened student engagement, enhanced concept mastery, and elevated academic accomplishments.

Lessons Learned: The successful incorporation of adaptive learning platforms necessitates alignment with curriculum objectives, continuous teacher training, and the fostering of a culture centered on data-informed decision-making. Collaborative efforts among educators, administrators, and technology developers are pivotal for seamless integration and maximizing the platform's impact on student learning outcomes.

Challenges Faced and Overcome: Hurdles encountered encompassed resistance to change, technical glitches, and apprehensions regarding data privacy. Overcoming these obstacles entailed the provision of extensive professional development opportunities for educators, prompt resolution of technical issues, and the implementation of robust measures to safeguard student data privacy.

Future Potential: Adaptive learning platforms hold significant promise for delivering personalized, data-driven instruction tailored to meet the diverse needs of students. Future advancements may entail the refinement of AI algorithms, integration with emerging technologies, and scalability to cater to broader student demographics.

Case Study 2: Implementation of Intelligent Tutoring Systems

Description: Intelligent tutoring systems harness AI to offer personalized guidance, feedback, and support to learners focusing on specific subjects or skill sets.

Success Story: At a university, the introduction of an intelligent tutoring system for computer programming courses proved highly beneficial. The system's ability to analyze students' coding proficiency, deliver real-time feedback and hints, and adjust the difficulty level of coding assignments resulted in noticeable enhancements in problem-solving capabilities, coding proficiency, and course completion rates.

Lessons Learned: Effective implementation of intelligent tutoring systems mandates collaboration among subject matter experts, instructional designers, and AI developers. Adherence to user-centered design principles, iterative feedback loops, and continual refinement processes are imperative for optimizing system usability and efficacy.

Challenges Faced and Overcome: Challenges encompassed usability issues, integration complexities with existing learning management systems, and scalability across diverse courses and disciplines. Overcoming these challenges involved rigorous user testing, interface redesign initiatives, and technical enhancements to bolster system performance and interoperability.

Future Potential: Intelligent tutoring systems harbor the potential to revolutionize education by offering personalized, adaptive learning experiences. Future developments may encompass augmented natural language processing capabilities, integration with virtual and augmented reality technologies, and expansion into novel subject domains.

Case Study 3: Utilization of Automated Grading Systems

Description: Automated grading systems leverage AI algorithms to evaluate and provide feedback on student assignments, quizzes, and assessments.

Success Story: A high school embraced an automated grading system for essays within

English language arts classes. Employing natural language processing, the system evaluated students' writing, assessed grammar, style, and content, and furnished personalized feedback. Teachers reported substantial time savings and enhanced grading consistency, enabling them to devote more attention to instructional planning and student assistance.

Lessons Learned: Successful deployment of automated grading systems necessitates the establishment of clear guidelines for rubric development, calibration, and feedback provision. Teachers assume a pivotal role in validating system-generated scores, supplementing feedback, and upholding assessment integrity.

Challenges Faced and Overcome: Challenges comprised algorithmic biases, linguistic intricacies, and the interpretability of AI-generated feedback. Addressing these challenges involved algorithm refinement, integration of teacher feedback into feedback generation processes, and training on interpreting and contextualizing AI-generated scores and comments.

Future Potential: Automated grading systems present opportunities for streamlined, scalable assessment practices conducive to personalized learning and prompt feedback delivery. Prospective developments may involve integration with plagiarism detection tools, expansion into other subject domains, and alignment with educational standards and objectives.

Case Study 4: Integration of Virtual Reality Simulations

Description: Virtual reality simulations leverage immersive VR environments to furnish hands-on learning experiences across diverse subject areas, including science, engineering, and healthcare.

Success Story: A medical school embraced virtual reality simulations for surgical training purposes. Students engaged in simulated surgical procedures within realistic virtual environments, leading to enhancements in procedural skills, decision-making prowess, and confidence levels in clinical settings. The simulations mitigated the necessity for cadaveric training while affording students a safe, repeatable learning milieu.

Lessons Learned: Effective integration of virtual reality simulations necessitates collaboration among educators, content developers, and VR technology specialists. Customization, interactivity, and realism emerge as critical factors in crafting immersive VR experiences conducive to learner engagement and skill acquisition.

Challenges Faced and Overcome: Challenges ranged from hardware and software limitations to content development expenses and curriculum integration complexities. Mitigating these challenges involved investments in VR equipment, collaboration with VR developers, and aligning simulations with learning objectives and competencies.

Future Potential: Virtual reality simulations hold promise for delivering experiential, immersive learning encounters bridging theoretical knowledge with practical application. Future advancements may involve the incorporation of haptic feedback devices, integration of multi-user collaboration features, and alignment with AI-driven adaptive learning systems.

Conclusion

The examination of real-world case studies underscores the manifold applications and potential of artificial intelligence in education. From adaptive learning platforms and intelligent tutoring systems to automated grading systems and virtual reality simulations, AI technologies proffer innovative solutions for enhancing teaching and learning outcomes.

Success stories underscore the benefits of AI integration, including personalized instruction, heightened student engagement, and improved learning outcomes. Lessons gleaned from case studies emphasize the significance of collaboration, user-centered design, and continuous evaluation in AI integration initiatives.

Challenges encountered and surmounted in AI deployment encompass technical hurdles, user acceptance issues, and ethical considerations. Addressing these challenges necessitates proactive measures, such as professional development initiatives, stakeholder engagement endeavors, and policy formulation.

Looking ahead, the future landscape of AI in education teems with potential for further innovation and advancement. As AI technologies evolve, stakeholders must remain vigilant in ensuring ethical utilization, safeguarding privacy, and fostering equitable access to AI-driven educational solutions. By leveraging insights derived from real-world case studies and embracing responsible AI integration practices, we can harness the transformative potential of AI to cultivate inclusive, engaging, and effective learning environments for all learners.

Chapter 15

Forecasting the Role of AI in Education

Introduction

The trajectory of education's future is profoundly intertwined with the advancements in artificial intelligence (AI). As AI continues its march forward, it holds the transformative potential to reshape educational methodologies, pioneer novel teaching paradigms, and surmount the hurdles facing the education sector. This chapter delves into burgeoning trends and technologies within AI, forecasts for the coming decade, the pivotal role of AI in shaping educational frameworks, and culminates with a rallying call to educators, policymakers, and stakeholders.

Emerging Trends and Technologies

1. **Natural Language Processing (NLP):** Progress in NLP is propelling AI systems towards a nuanced comprehension and generation of human language. This fosters conversational interfaces, virtual assistants, and intelligent tutoring systems, facilitating interactive dialogues with learners and offering tailored support.

2. **Emotion Recognition and Affective Computing:** AI's capacity to discern and respond to human emotions heralds implications for personalized learning, mental health assistance, and social-emotional learning initiatives in education. Emotion-sensitive systems can dynamically adjust instruction, offer empathetic feedback, and nurture student well-being.

3. **Immersive Technologies:** Virtual reality (VR), augmented reality (AR), and mixed reality (MR) present immersive educational landscapes wherein students can traverse virtual realms, simulate real-life scenarios, and engage with digital content in three-dimensional spaces.

4. **Data Analytics and Predictive Modeling:** AI-driven analytics delve into educational data, unraveling patterns, forecasting student trajectories, and guiding decision-making processes. Predictive models anticipate student needs, recommend interventions, and fine-tune instructional approaches to optimize learning outcomes.

Predictions for the Next Decade

1. **Personalized and Adaptive Learning:** AI's central role in personalized and adaptive learning ecosystems will burgeon, tailoring instruction, content, and assessments to individual student proclivities, preferences, and progression trajectories. Adaptive learning frameworks, fueled by AI algorithms, will chart bespoke learning pathways and bolster mastery-based learning initiatives.

2. **Lifelong Learning and Continuous Professional Development:** AI-fueled platforms for professional development will furnish educators with tailored learning experiences, empowering them to acquire new competencies, stay abreast of emerging trends, and evolve alongside educational paradigms throughout their careers.

3. **Global Collaboration and Access to Education:** AI-powered technologies will expedite global collaboration and broaden access to education, dismantling geographical barriers and furnishing equitable learning opportunities to learners across the

globe. Virtual classrooms, online learning platforms, and AI tutors will knit together learners and educators irrespective of borders, cultures, or languages.

4. **Ethical and Inclusive Design:** Ethical imperatives will underpin the design and deployment of AI technologies in education, spotlighting fairness, transparency, accountability, and privacy. Inclusive design ethos will ensure that AI-driven educational solutions remain accessible and equitable for all learners, regardless of their backgrounds or abilities.

AI's Role in Shaping Future Educational Models

1. **Shift towards Student-Centered Learning:** AI will embolden learners to seize the reins of their educational odyssey, nurturing autonomy, self-regulation, and metacognitive prowess. Student-centric educational frameworks will espouse personalized, experiential, and inquiry-based learning modalities,

empowering learners to explore, innovate, and create.

2. **Integration of AI into Curriculum and Pedagogy:** AI will seamlessly meld into curricular frameworks and pedagogical practices, amplifying educators' instructional arsenals and enriching learning experiences. Educators will harness AI tools and analytics to tailor instruction, differentiate learning activities, and furnish timely feedback to foster student growth and attainment.

3. **Expansion of Blended and Hybrid Learning Models:** Blended and hybrid learning schemas will gain ascendancy, amalgamating face-to-face instruction with online and virtual learning terrains. AI-powered technologies will fashion supple, adaptive learning milieus that cater to diverse learning styles, preferences, and exigencies.

4. **Redefined Roles for Educators:** Educators' mandates will transmute to embrace facilitation, mentorship, and coaching, eclipsing traditional didactic roles. Teachers will metamorphose into learning guides, mentors, and orchestrators of inquiry-driven, collaborative learning

exploits, leveraging AI technologies to bolster student learning and engagement.

Concluding Reflections and Urgent Call to Action

The vista of AI in education teems with promise, poised to metamorphose teaching and learning landscapes, widen the aperture of educational access, and incubate innovation and collaboration. However, the realization of this potential hinges upon concerted action and unwavering dedication from educators, policymakers, technology developers, and stakeholders. As we navigate the ever-shifting contours of AI in education, it is imperative to foreground ethical considerations, safeguard privacy prerogatives, and champion equitable access to AI-powered educational solutions. Educators must embrace a culture of lifelong learning, adapt to evolving educational paradigms, and harness the transformative potential of AI to amplify teaching efficacy and enhance student outcomes. Policymakers assume a pivotal mantle in erecting regulatory scaffolds, delineating ethical guideposts, and provisioning funding avenues conducive to the responsible integration of AI in education. By investing in research, infrastructure, and professional development initiatives, policymakers can engender AI technologies that redound to the advancement of education and societal well-being. Technology developers bear the onus of engineering AI-driven educational solutions that foreground user exigencies, uphold privacy strictures, and champion inclusivity and diversity. By fostering collaborations with educators, researchers, and stakeholders, technology developers can forge innovative, ethically robust AI technologies that enrich teaching and learning experiences for all learners. In summation, the future of AI in education gleams with promise, offering a crucible for innovation, collaboration, and positive transformation. Through concerted efforts and a steadfast embrace of AI's transformative potential, we can forge a future wherein education is not just accessible and equitable but also empowering, propelling learners towards success in an ever-evolving world.

www.ingramcontent.com/pod-product-compliance
Lightning Source LLC
La Vergne TN
LVHW051656050326
832903LV00032B/3841